SUN FUN

written and illustrated by
Caroline Arnold

an easy-read ACTIVITY book

FRANKLIN WATTS
New York/London/Toronto/Sydney
1981

For Matthew

Library of Congress Cataloging in Publication Data

Arnold, Caroline.
  Sun fun.

  (An easy-read activity book)
  Summary: Presents 10 projects that use energy
from the sun, including making a sun clock and sun
prints and cooking with the sun.
  1. Sunshine — Juvenile literature.   2. Sun —
Juvenile literature.   [1. Sun.   2. Handicraft]
I. Title.   II. Series: Easy-read activity book.
QC911.2.A76   551.5′271   81-98
ISBN 0-531-04312-6   AACR2

R.L. 2.3 Spache Revised Formula

CONTENTS

Did you know that you can:

tell time
by the sun?

cook
with the sun?

make pictures
with the sun?

The sun is a ball of fire in space.
It is far away from the earth.
But the **sun's rays** travel through space
to earth.
They give us different kinds of **energy**.
They give us light energy.
They give us heat energy.
Here are some projects you can do that
use energy from the sun.

ICE CUBE RACE

Your body has heat energy.
Does it have as much as the sun?
You can have a race with the sun.

You will need:
    two ice cubes the same size
    a small plate

Put one ice cube on the plate.
Put the plate in the sun.
The other ice cube is yours.
Try to melt it.
You can hold it, blow on it, or even put it in your mouth.
Which ice cube melts first—yours or the sun's?

A SUN CLOCK

The sun is our oldest clock.
Many years ago people learned to tell time
by the sun.
In the morning the sun rises in the east.
It makes long shadows that point west.

And at night the sun sets in the west.
Then it makes long shadows that point
east.

Here is an easy way that you can tell time
by the sun.

You will need:
  a paper plate
  two pencils
  a watch or clock

Find an open place outdoors where the
sun will shine all day.
Put the paper plate on the ground.
Make a hole in the middle of the plate
with a pencil.
Then put the pencil into the ground.
The pencil will hold the paper plate in
place.

It will also make a shadow.

Use the other pencil to draw a line along the shadow.

Write down the time on the line.

Look at the paper plate again in an hour.

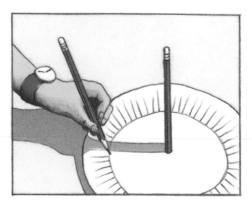 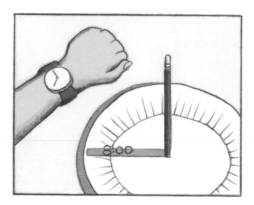

The shadow will have moved.

Draw a new line and mark down the new time. Each hour you can make a new line on the plate.

Each time write down what time it is.

 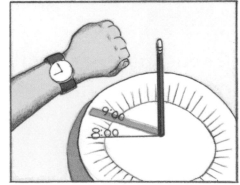

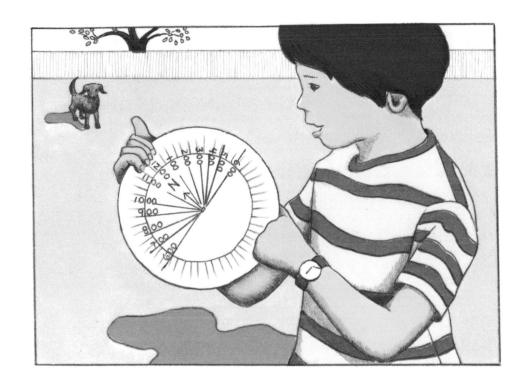

At the end of the day you will have a sun clock. Look at your lines.

Some are short. And some are long.

The shortest shadow is at noon.

When you want to use your sun clock again, point the line for the noon shadow north.

Where is the shadow of the pencil now? The lines on your sun clock will tell you what time it is.

SHADOW PUPPETS

The sun is like a giant light bulb in outer
space.
It lights up the earth.
When the sun shines on an object, it
makes a **shadow** behind the object.
Here is a way to give a puppet show with
shadows.

You will need:
    cardboard or heavy paper
    a pencil
    scissors
    ice cream sticks
    tape
    a sheet
    a rope
    a small table

First draw a puppet on the cardboard.
Remember that only the outline will show.
Then cut out the puppet.
You can cut holes for eyes.

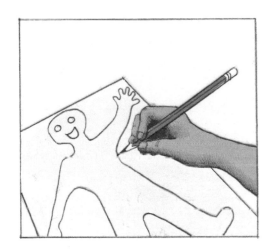 

Tape one of the sticks to the bottom of the puppet.

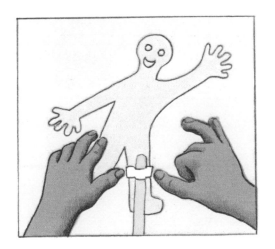 

For the puppet show, hang up the sheet
on the rope. Remember that the sun
must shine behind the sheet.
Ask your friends to face the sheet and the
sun.
Turn the table on its side behind the sheet.
Sit behind the table.
Hold the puppets above the table and near
the sheet.
Now you can give your puppet show.

SUN VISOR

Sunlight is made up of many kinds of rays.

We can see some of the rays.

A rainbow shows us the rays that we can see. It is red, orange, yellow, green, blue, and violet.

White light is a mixture of these rays.

But there are some parts of sunlight that you cannot see.

You cannot see **ultraviolet rays**.

Ultraviolet rays reach us even on cloudy days.

They help your body make vitamin D.

Ultraviolet rays also make your skin tan.
But too many can give you a sunburn.
Here is a kind of hat you can make.
It will keep your face from getting
sunburned.

You will need:
two paper plates   a piece of elastic, about
a pencil   12 inches (30.5 cm) long
scissors   a stapler

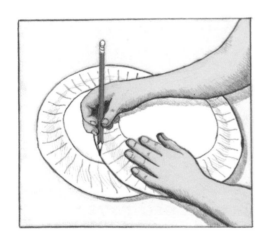 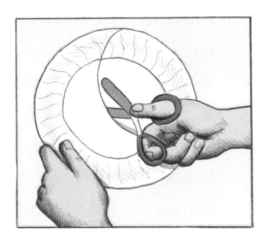

Partly cover one paper plate with the other
to make a moon shape on the bottom plate.
Draw around the edge of the top plate.
Then cut out the moon shape.
This will be the visor.

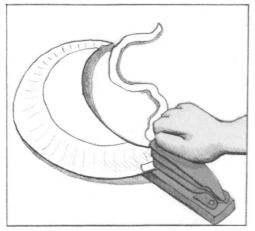 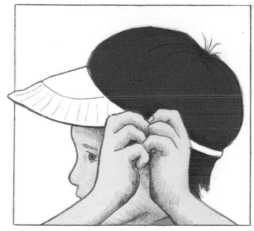

Staple the elastic to one end.

Adjust it to fit your head.

Staple the other end of the elastic to the other side.

Now you have a sun visor.

You can draw designs on the visor if you wish.

SUN PRINTS

You can make pictures with the sun.
Ultraviolet rays make studio proof paper
turn dark.
If you cover part of the paper, that part
will stay light.

You will need:
  a pencil
  tracing paper
  paper cutouts or objects
  studio proof (light-sensitive) paper (you can
    buy this where photographic equipment is sold)

Draw a picture on tracing paper.
Or you can make paper cutouts.
Or you can use objects to cover the paper.

  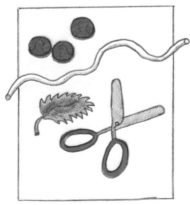

 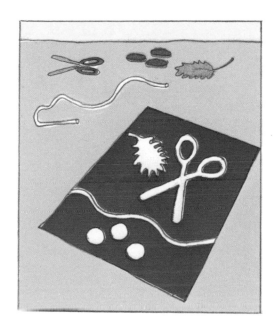

Put one of these things on the proof paper.
Put the proof paper in the sun.
You will see the proof paper turn dark.
It takes about one minute.
Then take everything out of the sun.
Take away your picture or objects.
You will see a print of it on the proof
paper.
You cannot keep this kind of print unless
you keep it in a dark place.
Any kind of light makes the whole print
turn dark after a while.

COOKING WITH THE SUN

Sunlight is warm.
It heats up the air around us.
It also heats up other things.
Here are two things you can "cook" in the
sun's heat.

Iced Tea

You will need:
    a clean jar with a lid
    water
    one or two tea bags

Fill the jar with cold water.
Add the tea bags.
Now put the lid on the jar.
Put the jar in the sun.
Wait about one hour.
Then look at the jar.
The tea will be brown.
And it will be warm.

Pour it over ice and
add a little sugar.
It will taste good.

Baked Apple

You will need:
    two clear plastic cups
    a small slice of apple
    clear plastic wrap
    tape
    a piece of black paper
    a paper towel
    tinfoil

Put the apple in the bottom of one cup.
Tightly wrap the cup in plastic wrap.

Tape the wrap in place.
Wrap the outside of the
cup in black paper
and tape it in place.

Put the towel in the second cup.
Then put the first cup inside the second.
The paper towel will be
between the two cups.

It helps to hold in
the heat.
Then wrap the foil around the cups to
make a cone shape.

The shiny side of the foil
should be on the inside
of the cone.
Tape the foil in place.
Now you have a sun
cooker.

Face the top of the cone toward the sun.
Wait about an hour.

When the skin of the
apple is brown,
it is done.
Then open the plastic
wrap.
Your apple will be hot.

It will taste good.

You can try cooking other things in your
sun cooker, too.

HOT ROCKS

Some things heat up better than others.
Try this experiment.

You will need:
    two rocks (about the size of your fist)
    white paint
    black paint

Paint one rock white.
Paint the other rock black.
Put both rocks in the sun.
Wait for an hour.

Then feel the rocks.

Which rock feels warmer?

The white rock **reflects** the sun's rays.

It stays cool.

The black rock **soaks up** the sun's rays.

It becomes warm.

To stay cool on a hot day, would you wear a dark shirt or a light one?

SUN REFLECTORS

Shiny things **reflect** sunlight best of all.
You can make reflectors with tinfoil.
With the reflector, you can make patterns
of light.

You will need:
   foil
   scissors
   cardboard
   glue

Cut out small pieces of foil.
Put them in patterns on the cardboard.
Glue them down.
Press out any wrinkles.
Now you have a reflector.

Hold it in the sun and watch it sparkle.

Shine it on a wall.

You will see your design.

Or hang it up in your room near a
window.

As the reflector turns in the sun, light will
shine around your room.

WATCHING A SOLAR ECLIPSE

Sometimes another planet or the moon
moves between the earth and the sun.
Then there is a giant shadow on the earth.
This is an **eclipse** of the sun, or **solar**
eclipse.
A solar eclipse does not happen very often.
Here is how to look at an eclipse.
Never look right at the sun.
It will hurt your eyes.

You can watch an eclipse safely if you
make a pinhole card.
The shape of the sun will shine through
the hole onto the ground.

You will need:
cardboard
a pin

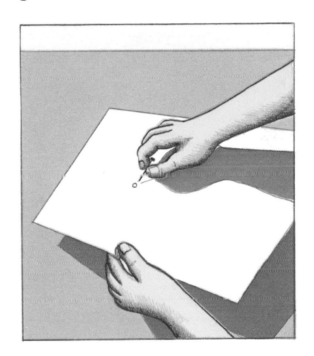

Make a very small hole in the cardboard
with the pin.
Hold the cardboard so that it faces the sun.
The sun will shine through the hole.
It will make a round spot of sunlight on
the ground.

During an eclipse the spot will not look round.

It will look as if part of the sun has been cut away.

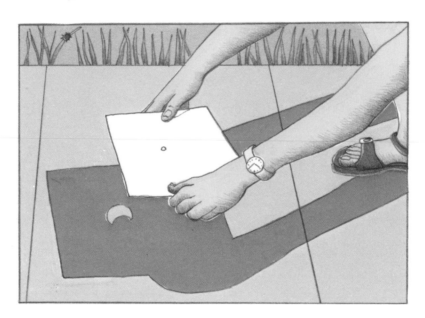

The spot will be round again when the eclipse is over.

In a full eclipse the shadow will cover the whole sun.

A full eclipse is rare.

But a part of an eclipse happens every few years.

MOVING PLANTS

Do you think that plants can move?
Try this experiment to find out.

You will need:
   a plant
   a sunny window

Put the plant in a sunny window.

Turn it so the leaves do not face the sun.

Look at it again in an hour or two.

Which way are the leaves facing?

Plants need sunlight to grow.

They use sunlight to make their own food.

Plants will turn their leaves to reach the
sun.

We need the sun, too.
Without the sun there would be no life on earth.
We need the sun for warmth.
And we need it for light.
We also have fun in the sun.